SCHIRMER'S LIBRARY
OF MUSICAL CLASSICS

Vol. 2122

THE BAROQUE CELLO COLLECTION

10 Pieces by 9 Composers

for Cello and Piano

ISBN 978-1-4950-5076-3

G. SCHIRMER, Inc.

DISTRIBUTED BY

HAL•LEONARD®
CORPORATION

7777 W. BLUEMOUND RD. P.O. BOX 13819 MILWAUKEE, WI 53213

www.musicsalesclassical.com
www.halleonard.com

Contents

Sonata in G minor
BWV 1029

Johann Sebastian Bach
(1685–1750)

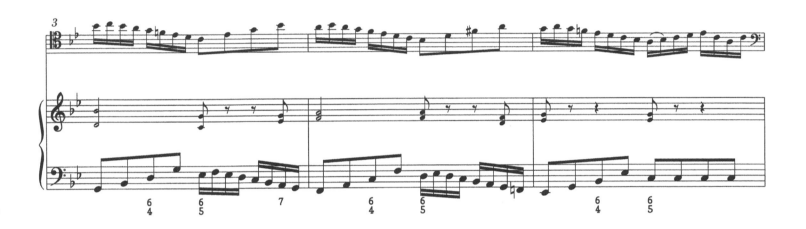

Adagio

Allegro

Sonata in A Major

Edited by Janos Starker

Luigi Boccherini
(1743–1805)

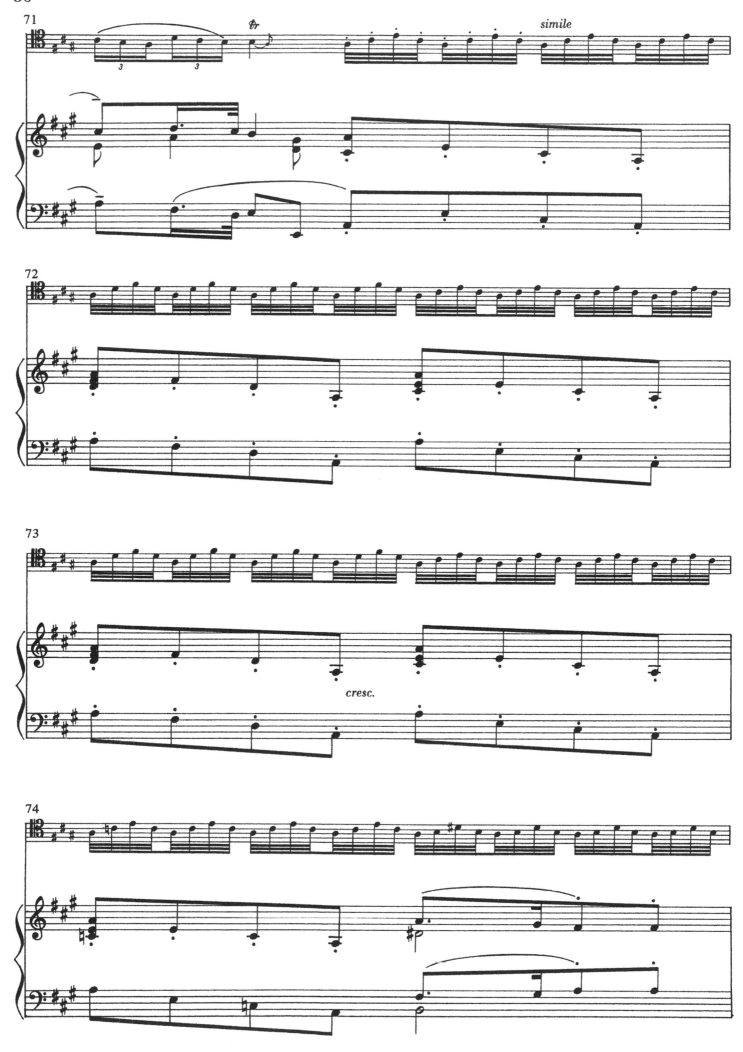

Sonata in D minor

Edited by Janos Starker

Arcangelo Corelli
(1653–1713)

ALLEMANDA

Allegro

SARABANDA

GIGA

Sonata in D Major

Edited by Janos Starker

Pietro Locatelli
(1695–1764)

55

MINUETTO

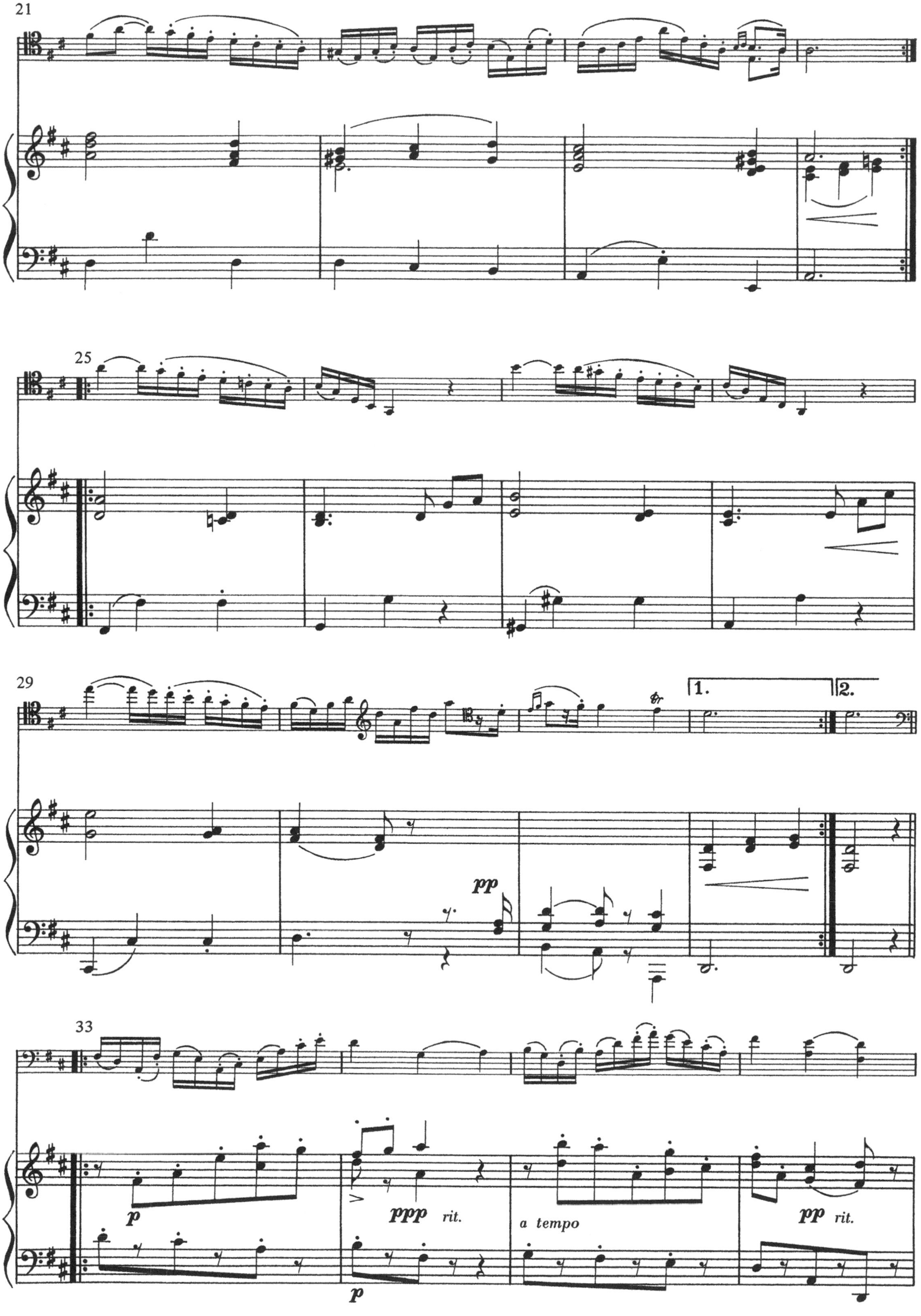
21
25
29
1.
2.
pp
33
p
ppp rit.
a tempo
pp rit.
p

64

Sonata in E minor

Benedetto Marcello
(1686–1739)

Sonata in G Major

Edited by Janos Starker

Giovanni Battista Sammartini
(c.1700–1775)

Sonata in D minor

Alessandro Scarlatti
(1660–1725)

Realization by Analee Bacon

Allegretto

90

Largo

A tempo giusto

*Scarlatti has an E here.

Sonata in E Major

Edited by Janos Starker

Giuseppe Valentini
(1681–1753)

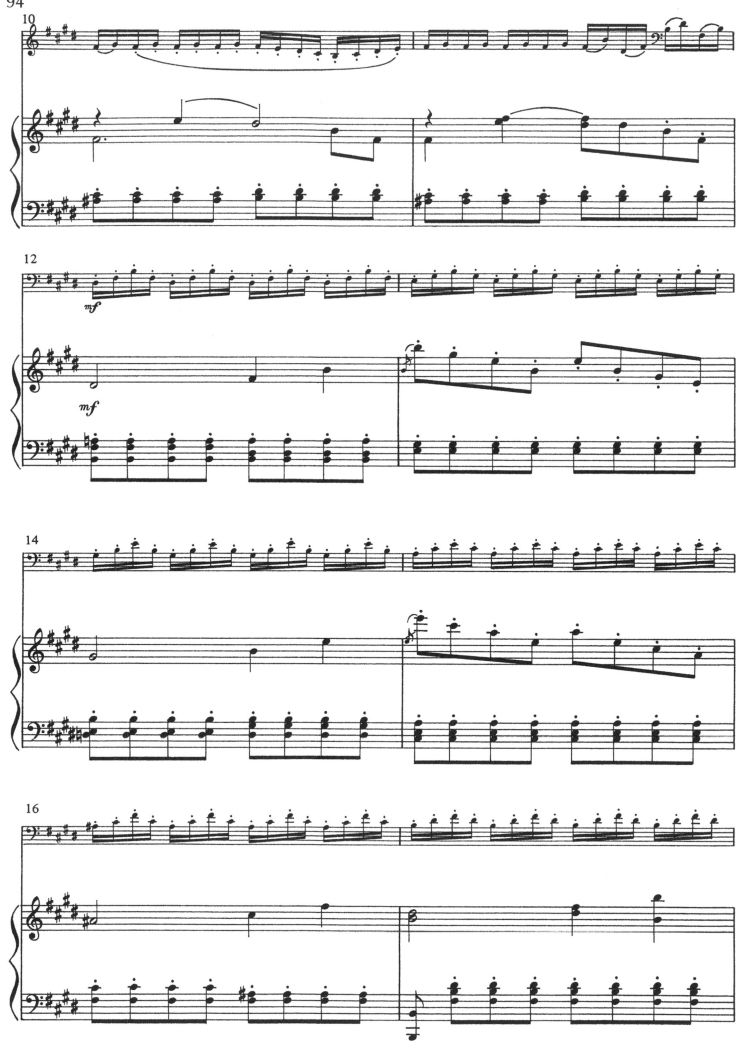

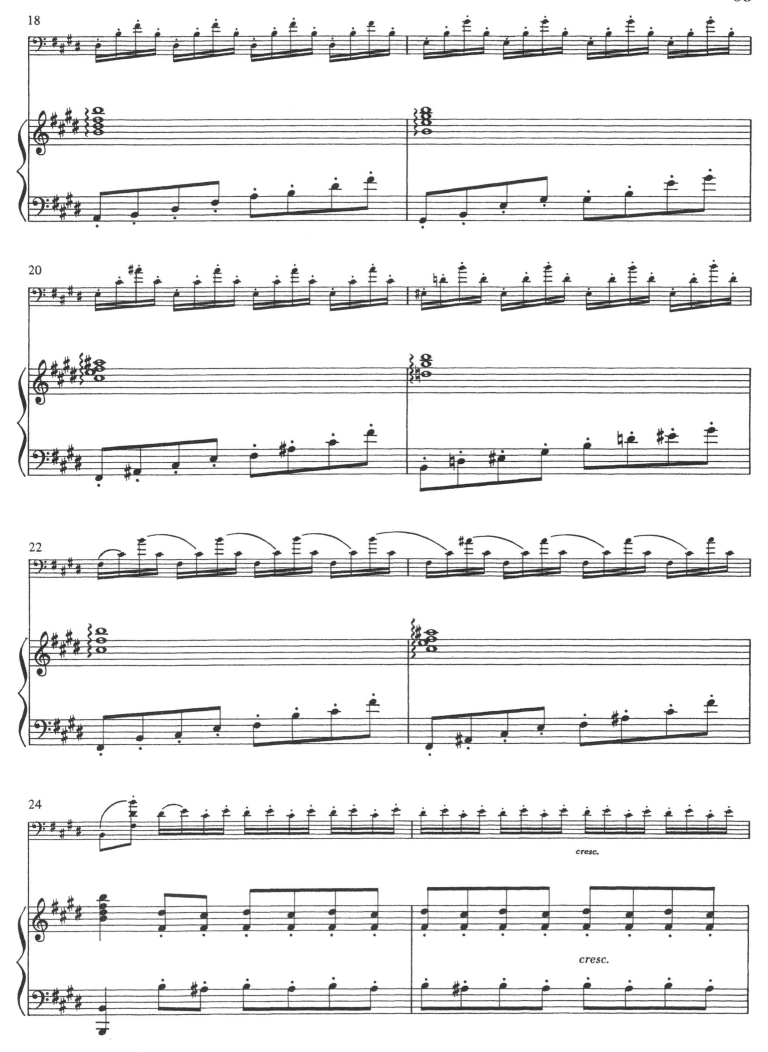

Sonata in A minor

Antonio Vivaldi
(1678–1741)

Allegro (energico)

Allegro (Allegretto moderato, poco giocondo)